W9-BYM-015

FORESTS

A FACT-FILLED COLORING BOOK

Bettina Dudley

Illustrated by Helen I. Driggs

RUNNING PRESS

PHILADELPHIA, PENNSYLVANIA

Copyright © 1989 by Running Press.
Printed in the United States of America. All rights reserved
under the Pan-American and International Copyright Conventions.

*This book may not be reproduced in whole or in part in any form or by any means, electronic or mechanical, including
photocopying, recording, or by any information storage and retrieval system now known or hereafter invented, without
written permission from the publisher.*

Canadian representatives: General Publishing Co., Ltd.,
30 Lesmill Road, Don Mills, Ontario M3B 2T6

International representatives: Worldwide Media Services, Inc.,
115 East Twenty-third Street, New York, New York 10010

9 8 7 6 5 4 3 2 1

Digit on the right indicates the number of this printing.

ISBN 0–89471–782–0

Cover design by Toby Schmidt
Interior design by Liz Vogdes
Cover illustrations by Helen I. Driggs
Interior illustrations by Helen I. Driggs
Poster illustration by Helen I. Driggs
Poster copyright © Running Press Book Publishers
Printed by Chernay Printing, Inc., Coopersburg, Pennsylvania
Typography by Commcor Communications Corporation,
Philadelphia, Pennsylvania
This book may be ordered by mail from the publisher.
Please add $2.50 for postage and handling for each copy.
But try your bookstore first!
Running Press Book Publishers
125 South Twenty-second Street
Philadelphia, Pennsylvania 19103

CONTENTS

INTRODUCTION

This is a book about forests—how they began long ago, what keeps them growing, what kinds of forests there are today, and why they must be preserved for tomorrow.

Forests are found in fantastic variety all around the world. You may be able to name a few famous ones, such as the California redwood forest or the bamboo forest of China. But as you look at and color the pictures in this book, you may be surprised to see how many kinds of forests there are.

To many American children, a typical forest is one that blazes into color in the fall. If you have lived on or visited the East Coast of the United States, you probably have seen a forest like that. It is full of maples and other trees with broad, green leaves that turn bright red, orange, or yellow each autumn and fall off when winter begins.

If you were to visit such a forest, you might see a blue jay building its nest on the high branches or a squirrel scurrying in and out of its home in a dead trunk. Food for each of them is all around. The blue jay eats insects, and the squirrel eats seeds and fruits from many different plants.

When scientists study the plants and animals of a single forest, they see that each plant and animal depends on one or more of the others in an important way. Scientists say that the plants and animals are *interdependent*. Any place where plants and animals are interdependent is called an *ecosystem*.

The planet Earth is the largest ecosystem. An aquarium with fish, snails, and live plants is a very small ecosystem. A forest is an ecosystem, whether that forest covers a few acres or hundreds of square miles.

PART ONE
HOW THE FORESTS BEGAN

What Is a Forest?

What makes a forest different from another community of plants and animals—such as a desert, grassland, or tundra? We usually recognize a forest by its trees.

Most forests have trees, but some do not. Two examples are the ''tree fern'' forests that grow in the tropics and the giant kelp forests that grow on the bottom of the Pacific Ocean.

Tree ferns look a lot like trees, but they are not trees at all. They are ferns that grow as tall as trees. Giant kelp, a brown seaweed that grows off the western coast of the United States, looks somewhat like a tree in that it has a thick stem with leaf-like blades growing along it, and a root-like extension at the bottom that holds it to the ocean floor. Some giant kelp plants grow to more than 300 feet—as tall as a good-sized redwood tree!

The tree fern and the giant kelp are not trees because they lack two things every tree has: wood and seeds. Trees make wood from a special tissue called *cambium*. And trees make seeds from which new trees will grow.

A forest of trees

Animals All Around

Every forest is filled with animals, most of which we never notice. A squirrel or a blue jay might scold us for being there, but we could easily walk right by a quietly sitting rabbit or a robin perched on its nest.

Think of all the creatures you could see on one big oak tree. A black snake might climb up into its branches looking for a meal in a bird's nest. A hawk might alight on the uppermost branch. Raccoons and opossums, maybe even a bobcat, might pass the daylight hours hidden in the tree, safe from their enemies. A bat could be sleeping there during the day, too, hanging upside down until nightfall. Squirrels could use the tree as part of their daily journey through the treetops, and the branches could be filled with songbirds.

Near all these animals are hundreds and hundreds—and hundreds!—of smaller creatures. Butterflies, caterpillars, beetles, ants, bees—the list could go on and on.

These are all animals we can see. With a microscope, we could see thousands more. We could see tiny insects, tinier worms, and even animals that have only one cell each!

An oak tree can be as busy as any street in New York. If it is a big oak tree, it is hundreds of years old. Think how many lives have been lived and how much has happened on just one tree!

ANIMAL TRACKER

The raccoon is a very intelligent animal found throughout most of the United States and Canada. The raccoon may belong to the same family of creatures as the giant panda—both wear a "mask" of black fur around their eyes.

The raccoon's beautiful coat has made it the target of humans, who for centuries have hunted it for its fur.

Raccoons have lots of curiosity, and can open latches and containers with their paws. They are common visitors to campsites, suburban garbage cans, and farmers' chicken coops.

Nature in Balance

It's really hard to realize how many living creatures make their homes in just one tree, and even harder to imagine all the life in a whole forest. Probably no one has ever tried to figure out the total number of plants and animals, but scientists have studied some forest animals in great detail.

From these studies we have come to realize that the total number of animals in any forest must be very large. Here's one example.

Scientists have studied forest warblers, and have learned a lot about how they live. These tiny birds spend the winter in the lowland forests of Central America, and then fly thousands of miles north to the forests of eastern North America. There they build their nests, lay their eggs, and raise their young.

It takes about ten days from the time the eggs hatch until the baby birds are ready to leave the nest. During that time, the parent birds bring them little green caterpillars that live in the forest eating leaves. In each nest, there are usually between three and five baby birds. Can you guess how many caterpillars the baby warblers in just one nest eat in ten days? Are you ready? *One thousand and seven hundred (1,700) caterpillars!* That's a lot of caterpillars—170 caterpillars every day, to be exact.

This story shows us how members of a forest depend upon one another. Trees provide places for warblers to nest. They also provide leaves for caterpillars to eat. Warblers eat some of the caterpillars, so the caterpillars don't eat all the leaves of the trees.

Trees need warblers—and both warblers and caterpillars need trees. With a natural balance of trees, birds, and insects, all three life forms can thrive.

The First Forests

Long ago, there were no forests anywhere in the world.

The first living things we know about were single cells, most of them so tiny you would need a microscope to see them. Imprints of these cells appear on rocks that scientists believe are 3½ *billion* years old. Such an imprint is called a fossil.

The fossil record of life on Earth suggests that animal life, in its most primitive form, did not exist until 1.4 billion years ago—more than 2 billion years after the beginning of plant life. Modern humans appeared on the scene a mere 200,000 years ago.

Scientists believe that in a process called *evolution,* early life forms were replaced by the life forms we see today. Evolution is change taking place over many years, with each generation passing on changes to the next.

It took billions of years for some of those trees to evolve. The first trees we know of appeared about 400 million years ago. It was another 165 million years before the earliest dinosaurs walked the earth.

Some of the first forests developed in swamps. Primitive plants such as the horsetail and club moss grew close together and reached as high as 100 feet into the sky—taller than a 10-story building!

Many kinds of single-cell plants survive today. For example, you can often see *algae,* the most common, as a green film floating on the top of a still pond. Some kinds of horsetail and club moss survive, too, though today they usually grow only a few inches tall, and even if you saw a thousand of them together, you wouldn't think they were a forest! Most other kinds of plants and animals that lived in those early swamp forests are no longer living.

The fossil record is like a book with many pages missing. We can know only part of the story of the history of life, because only some plants and animals become fossils. So although we do know a lot about ancient forms of life, we will never know exactly what ancient forests were like.

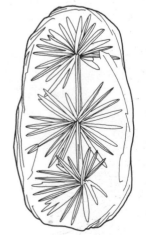

fossilized giant horsetail

The Petrified Forest

A fossil is the hardened imprint or remains of a plant or animal that lived long ago. If you have ever visited a natural history museum, you probably have seen fossils of dinosaurs or other prehistoric animals on display. Perhaps you saw a dinosaur footprint, preserved in ancient rock as though the animal had stepped into wet cement. Or you may have seen a few fossil bones wired together with artificial bones to show what the skeleton of such an animal must have looked like.

A scientist who studies dinosaurs can study footprints and a few bones and figure out not only what the animal looked like, but when it lived and what it ate. In the same way, a scientist who studies plants can study fossil remains and figure out a lot about the vegetation in prehistoric forests.

Some plant fossils are tiny, even microscopic, such as the imprints of single-cell algae. But some plant fossils are huge.

If you were to visit the Petrified Forest National Park in Arizona, you would see the hardened remains of gigantic cone-bearing trees that lived in the days of the dinosaur. These fossils look like the huge logs they once were, but feel like the rocks they have become. In the millions of years that have passed since these trees were alive, the living tissues in them have been replaced by quartz.

Forests made up of the kinds of trees found in the Petrified Forest National Park probably looked a lot like the redwood forests of today. The trees were so big that even the big animals living among them seemed small by comparison.

Two Types of Trees

During the 160 million years that dinosaurs roamed the earth, many new kinds of trees developed. By the time the last of the dinosaurs were gone, about 65 million years ago, all trees could be divided into two basic types.

One type has seeds inside a fruit, such as an apple or a banana—or even a maple!

You may have seen the fruits of a maple tree as they fly off a tree in an early summer breeze, their delicate wings causing them to spin or float briefly as they descend. You may have pulled one apart and stuck it on the tip of your nose. If you've never thought of it as a fruit, that's because you're not a botanist.

"Botanist" is the name for a scientist who studies plants. A botanist who thinks of fruit thinks of the part of a plant that encloses its seeds. Acorns or avocados, chestnuts or cherries, they're all fruits to a botanist.

The second basic type of tree has naked seeds. A pine tree is a good example of this type. If you can find a pine cone that is still attached to the tree, and look closely at the upper surface of its scales, you may see the pine seeds—if a squirrel hasn't found them first and eaten them!

A squirrel only has to separate the scales of the pine cone to expose the seeds. A mouse hungry for maple seeds has to chew away the covering to get a meal.

PART TWO
WHAT KEEPS FORESTS GROWING?

Leaves

How many shapes and sizes of leaves can you find on forest trees? One good answer would be "lots and lots"!

A leaf can be simple, with a smooth, oval outline. It can be shaped like your open hand. It can have sharp spines, or rows of teeth along its edges. A leaf can be compound, which means that it is made up of several smaller leaflets.

A leaf can be very small or *very* big. The leaf of a tree fern can be 10 feet long. A leaf can be thin as a pine needle or two feet wide.

You can see the variety of leaves for yourself by making a leaf collection. Go to a garden, park, or forest and carefully pick a leaf from several different plants. Layer your leaves between sheets of newspaper and put a heavy book on top of the pile. In a few days, the leaves will be dry and you can glue them onto a sheet of plain or colored paper to create an interesting picture.

No matter what their size or shape, all leaves have the same job. They make food for the plant.

The part of a leaf that enables it to make food is the same part that makes a leaf green. It is a pigment called *chlorophyll* (CLORE-uh-fill). This amazing substance absorbs energy from sunlight so that the plant can make sugar from water and air.

Here's how it works. Plants absorb water by their roots. Leaves take from the air what we exhale: carbon dioxide. With the help of chlorophyll, green plants use energy from the sun, in a series of chemical reactions, to make sugar from carbon dioxide and water. This process, which makes it possible for plants to grow, is called *photosynthesis* (fo-to-SIN-thuh-sis), which means "making with light."

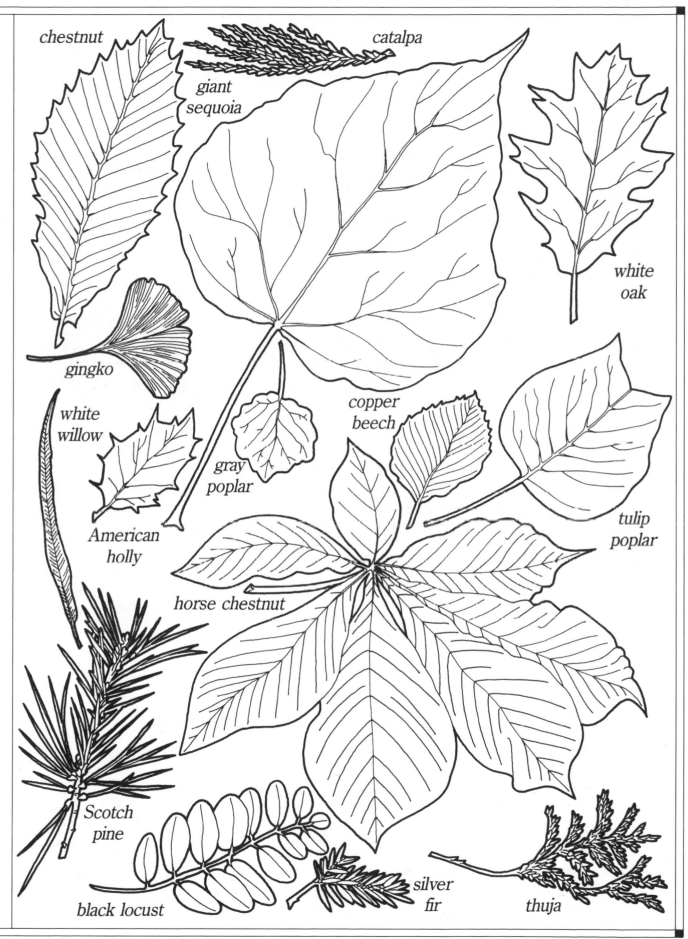

chestnut

giant sequoia

catalpa

white oak

gingko

white willow

gray poplar

American holly

copper beech

tulip poplar

horse chestnut

Scotch pine

black locust

silver fir

thuja

Fall Colors

In spring, some forests put on a quiet show of beauty for those who go to see the carpet of wildflowers below the still-bare branches of oak and maple trees.

But by September or early October, the show of color is far from quiet as leaves take on their autumn hues. This spectacle of color is at its best in New England, and along the tops of mountain ranges southward, all the way down to Georgia and Alabama. Many people drive for hundreds of miles to see scarlet maples and golden oaks framed against the blue sky of autumn.

Have you ever wondered how fall color comes to be? Sometimes it seems to just appear one crisp October day as a blaze of color. The amazing fact is that these glowing red, orange, yellow, and brown colors were always there in the leaves of spring and summer, but were masked by the green color.

That green color is the special pigment called chlorophyll. It is the green of all plants, and plants need it to produce their own food. All summer long, trees with green leaves produce their food and grow. In the fall, as the days grow shorter and cooler, the chlorophyll pigment breaks up and fades. As this happens, we can see new and glorious colors in every leaf.

Cool summer greens and sparkling autumn beauty—how lucky can we be!

Roots

When you look at an oak tree, or any tree in a forest, you see only part of it. An oak tree's roots, reaching down into the soil from the base of the trunk, number many more than its branches—perhaps five or six times more. The very foundations of a forest floor are its roots.

Scientists don't know the size of an average tree's root system because no one has ever been able to dig up an entire system. Not only do the roots go deep and far, there are millions of them.

If the roots of a large oak tree could be placed end to end, they would stretch for hundreds of miles!

The thick, brown roots you may have seen on or near the surface of the soil are old and mostly provide support—one of two important jobs performed by roots. Trees are naturally top-heavy and, like tall buildings, they need a strong foundation to anchor them and keep them from toppling over.

Thin roots branch off from thick ones, and still thinner rootlets branch off from them. The rootlets—no thicker than string at their growing tips—are covered with thousands of tiny hairs, each one the width of a single cell. These root hairs absorb water and minerals. That's the second important job performed by roots.

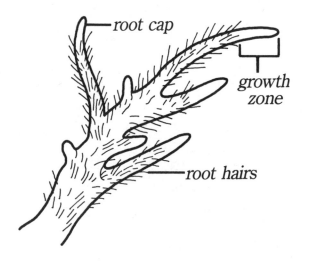

Water goes up through the trunk to the leaves, where some of it is used to make food for the tree. Much of the rest of the water evaporates. Hundreds of gallons of water may evaporate from a single tree on one warm, sunny day. To make food and to keep from drying up, a tree needs a constant supply of water. Since young roots and root hairs are the only part of a tree that can absorb water, they have to do a very

The strong root cap is pushed through soil.
Tiny root hairs (the width of 1 cell) absorb water.

continued on page 28

New leaves form every year, and rapid growth occurs in the branches.

Twigs, like roots, grow from the tips, and branches get thicker every year.

Trunk thickens each year.

Roots grow thicker and longer each year.

Root caps grow at tips, and hairs form behind caps.

Roots, *continued*

good job, and there have to be a lot of them.

You can see a root system for yourself by digging up a small weed. Dig in a circle at least a few inches from the weed's stem and down as deep as your trowel will go. Put the weed and all the soil you dug out with it in a shallow pan filled with water. As the water loosens the soil from the roots, you'll be able to see what a large root system even a little weed has. You could put the weed in a glass of water and watch to see if the roots grow during the next few days.

If you want to see root hairs, place some radish seeds on a damp paper towel in a bowl. Cover the bowl with plastic wrap to keep the towel moist. You'll probably need to sprinkle the towel with a little water every day. In a few days, the root should start to grow. It will look fuzzy because of all its root hairs.

Plants that Live on Air

You may be surprised to learn that some plants do very well without soil. These plants, called "air plants" or *epiphytes* (EP-uh-fites), grow on other plants—but not just any plants. They must live in an area that gets lots of moisture from rain, mist, or fog, and in a minute you'll see why.

A plant that roots in soil has an anchor, to keep it from blowing away and to keep its above-ground growth from toppling over. It also has access to water and minerals, to be absorbed when needed.

PLANT FACTS

Two kinds of plants live in trees high above the ground: parasites and epiphytes.

The mistletoe plant (shown here) is a parasite. It uses nutrients from trees, weakening the trees—and, in some cases, killing them.

Orchids and Spanish moss are epiphytes. These plants cling to a tree with their roots, or drape over branches. These plants get nutrients from rainwater, leaf litter, and other organic debris in the air.

Mistletoe roots enter the bark and wood of their host.

All plants must have support and nourishment to survive. How do you suppose air plants get them?

First of all, air plants need very little support because they do not grow very tall. An air plant that has roots, such as an orchid, may grasp a branch or cling to the bark of a tree. An air plant such as Spanish moss drapes itself over the branches of a cypress tree like grayish-green lace.

Air plants grow only in places that get lots of moisture, such as a rain forest or a swamp. Without roots to tap water in the soil, they need an almost constant supply of water from the air. And they need a way to store water for use when the air is dry.

Air plants such as orchids, considered by many people to be among the most beautiful flowers in the world, have tissues inside their roots that act like sponges. Other air plants have such sponges in their stems or leaves. Still others have leaves that form cups to catch and hold water. The leaves of some large plants which are related to

(continued on page 32)

Spanish moss

Plants that Live on Air, *continued*

pineapples form a bucket that can hold more than a gallon of water!

The minerals that most plants get from the soil, air plants get in other ways. Some minerals come from the dead cells of plants above them. Some minerals come from the dead leaves of other plants that fall onto the air plant and are cradled there in a basket formed by its leaves until they decompose. Some minerals are found in debris that blows or falls into the nooks and crannies of the supporting tree. Some minerals settle on the air plants from dust in the atmosphere. And some are carried to the air plants in seeds and other plant material deposited by insects that visit or nest in these plants.

Air plants, like all plants and animals, get what they need to survive from the ecosystem to which they belong. But, like all plants and animals, their continued survival depends on the health of that ecosystem.

Orchids

Plants with Flowers

Some plants have flowers, and some plants have cones. Plants with flowers are called *angiosperms* (AN-gee-o-sperms).

There are hundreds and hundreds and hundreds of kinds of flowers: roses and orchids and tulips and buttercups and daffodils—all flowers, and all looking very different.

Even though they look so different, they are all based on the same design. On the very outside of a typical flower is a whorl of sepals. These are often green. Next comes a whorl of petals—red in red roses, yellow in yellow buttercups, other colors in other flowers. The petals are the showy part of a flower.

Inside the petals are *stamens.* These produce pollen. Have you ever seen a bee whose legs are covered with yellow pollen? That pollen came from flowers the bee was visiting.

In the very center of a flower is the *pistil.* At the base of the pistil is the *ovary,* where seeds develop. The ovary of any flower develops into a fruit that protects the seeds until they are old enough to form new plants themselves.

Rose hips, bananas, apples—these are all fruits that protect the seeds to make more roses, bananas, and apples. Flowering trees in a forest produce fruits, too, even though their fruits don't look much like your lunchtime banana!

Plants with Cones

Pine trees and other plants that have cones are in the category that scientists call *gymnosperms* (JIM-no-sperms). Just as flowers can look very different from one another, cones look very different from each other, too.

Like flowers, all cones share a basic plan, even if they look very different.

The big cones that catch our attention on trees are female cones. Each cone has many scales. On the upper surface of each scale are two small outgrowths that can develop into seeds.

Male cones are much smaller than the showy female cones, and they don't stay on the tree for many months, as females do. Tiny, light pollen grains are carried from male cones by the wind. When these grains of pollen reach a female cone and fertilize the ovules on the scales, seeds will be formed.

Next time you have a chance to walk in a forest, look down at the ground instead of up at the trees growing over you. You may be able to find seedlings—young plants that sprout after seeds fall to the forest floor and start to grow there. The next generation of trees is on its way!

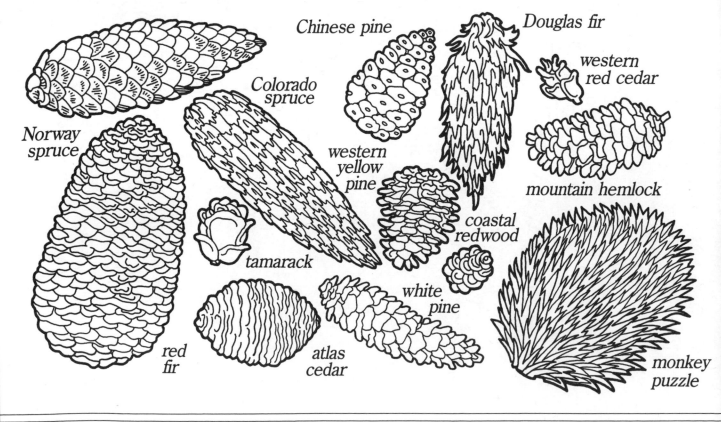

Chinese pine

Douglas fir

western red cedar

Colorado spruce

Norway spruce

western yellow pine

mountain hemlock

coastal redwood

tamarack

white pine

red fir

atlas cedar

monkey puzzle

The Food Chain

Every forest is a web of relationships among the plants and animals that live there together.

Scientists study these relationships. They sometimes think of the plants and animals in a forest as the individual parts that together make up the *food chain.* Members of the food chain can be divided into three groups: producers, consumers, and decomposers.

Green plants are the world's producers. With the help of the green pigment chlorophyll, they make their own food from water, air, and sunlight.

Animals are consumers. They can't make their own food, so they eat plants or other animals. Some animals eat only plants. They are called *herbivores* (URB-eh-vores). Some animals eat only other animals. They are called *carnivores.* And some animals eat both plants and animals. These animals are called *omnivores.* (If you want to see a really interesting omnivore, look in the mirror!)

Bacteria and fungi are decomposers. They break down dead plants and animals into simple nutrients that go back into the soil to nourish living plants. This completes the food chain.

In any forest, you can easily see a few links in the food chain.

In a northern forest, for example, you might see a shallow lake with water plants that feed gigantic moose and tiny snails. The snails are food for fish. The fish are food for water birds such as the common loon.

In an oak forest, you could see oak leaves providing food for little green caterpillars, which in turn are eaten by birds such as forest warblers.

Each link in a food chain is vital to all other links. When one link is weakened or removed by human carelessness, plants and animals from one end of the chain to the other can be harmed.

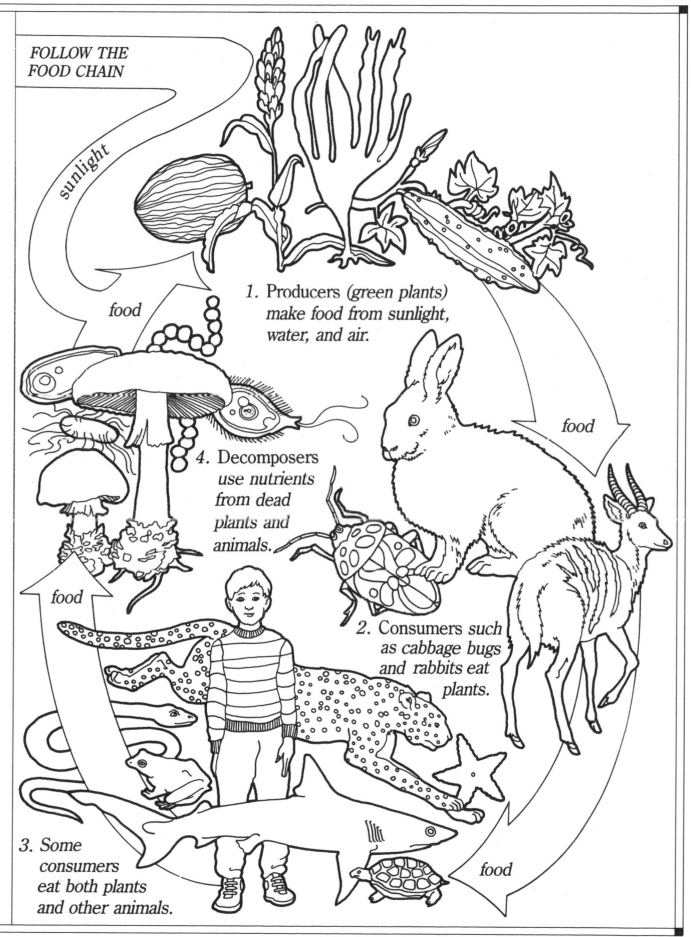

FOLLOW THE
FOOD CHAIN

sunlight

food

1. Producers (green plants)
make food from sunlight,
water, and air.

food

4. Decomposers
use nutrients
from dead
plants and
animals.

food

2. Consumers such
as cabbage bugs
and rabbits eat
plants.

3. Some
consumers
eat both plants
and other animals.

food

Layers of Forest Growth

When we think of forests, we often think of the big trees, the large animals, and the brightly colored birds that live there. Yet all forests are made up of many more plants and animals than the ones that are so easy to see.

Forests have several layers of plants. You can easily see this in the spring, before the leaves of the taller trees have developed fully. Then you can see the outline of the trunk and the branches forming a crown at the top of each tree.

Underneath these trees is a second layer that you may not have noticed before. If you live where there are dogwood trees, however, you may have noticed these because they have beautiful showy white or pink flowers in late April and early May. The dogwood trees grow only about 20 to 30 feet tall. Together with other small trees, such as hollies, they make a second layer far below the crowns of the taller trees.

A third layer is from ground level and up to about five to six feet high. This layer is made up of lots of plants—ferns, mosses, all the spring flowers, grasses, and small shrubs such as blueberries.

dogwood blossom

Nearly all forests have a layered structure, but the number of layers is different in different climates. In the rain forests of the tropics, you would have a hard time seeing the layers at any time of the year. A rain forest may have five or six layers, each layer so full and lush that together they look like a solid green hedge reaching from the ground to the sky.

canopy
layer

understory
layer

ground
layer

Wildflowers

Most of the flowers that bloom in a forest come and go so quickly that you may never have seen them. But if you look in the right place at the right time, you will find them and be glad you did.

A good place to find many of these wildflowers is a forest of *deciduous* trees (trees that lose their leaves in winter), especially near a river. Rivers often overflow their banks during rains and enrich the nearby soil. This makes a wonderful place for wildflowers to grow.

The best time to look for wildflowers is in the early spring, before the trees leaf out and before the poison ivy starts to grow—and that makes it easy and pleasant to walk around and take a close look.

If you do find yourself in the right place at the right time, you may come upon a delicate carpet of colorful forest wildflowers. Some are simple in shape and some are quite ornate. Their names are delightful: spring beauty, dogtooth violet, ladyslipper orchid, Dutchman's breeches, columbine, bluebell, trillium, Jack-in-the-pulpit. As you color the pictures of wildflowers, see if you can imagine how each one might have gotten its common name.

When you see these flowers in a forest, you know that they weren't in flower yesterday, and soon they will be gone. Their short flowering season will end and their green leaves will be hard to find among the bolder leaves of vines and bushes. Their special beauty lasts only a few days, awaiting those who know how to look for it.

Sometimes these same plants are grown in home gardens, so we don't always have to visit a forest to see them. If you know someone who has a flower garden, ask if any wildflowers grow there.

dog-tooth
violet

Virginia
bluebells

columbine

trillium

Dutchman's breeches

periwinkle

Jack-in-the-pulpit

skunk cabbage

dewdrop

How Old Is That Tree?

You may have wondered, "How can anyone really know how old a tree is?" It's a very good question, and it has an interesting answer.

Scientists know that the oldest living tree is a bristlecone pine more than 4,500 years old. They know that some sequoia trees in California are about 3,000 years old. How do they know? The trunk of the tree tells them.

Trees grow in two directions at once. As they grow taller, they also grow wider. Each year a tree adds new tissue at the tips of its branches. At the same time it grows a layer of woody tissue all the way around its trunk. In the spring, when growth is fastest, the cells of this new wood are very large.

You'll be glad to know that scientists have invented a tool to find out how old a tree is without having to cut it down.

A small metal tube is driven into a tree to obtain a sample of the wood, from the bark to the heartwood at the trunk's center. The sample is studied in the laboratory to discover patterns in weather and the extent of fire and insect damage in past years.

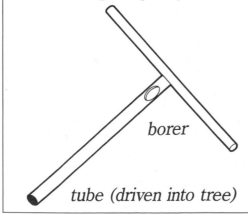

borer

tube (driven into tree)

Later, the rate of growth slows, and the cells become smaller. During the wintertime there is no growth at all, and no new cells. The place where a ring of small cells meets a ring of large cells marks the passage of a year. (In the tropics, where there are not such sharp contrasts between seasons, growth is much more even, and these rings are not obvious.)

When a tree has been cut down, we can look at growth rings, and we can count them. Because growth slows during the fall, stops during the winter, and then starts again in the spring, it is easy to see where each year's growth begins and ends by looking at the size of the cells. In a year with lots of rain, the tree may have grown more than in most other years, and the ring will be wider than its neighbors. In a very dry year there may be very little growth, and the ring will be narrow. So when you look at the flat surface of a cut log, you can tell how old the tree was by counting its rings, and you can also know a little about the weather conditions as it grew.

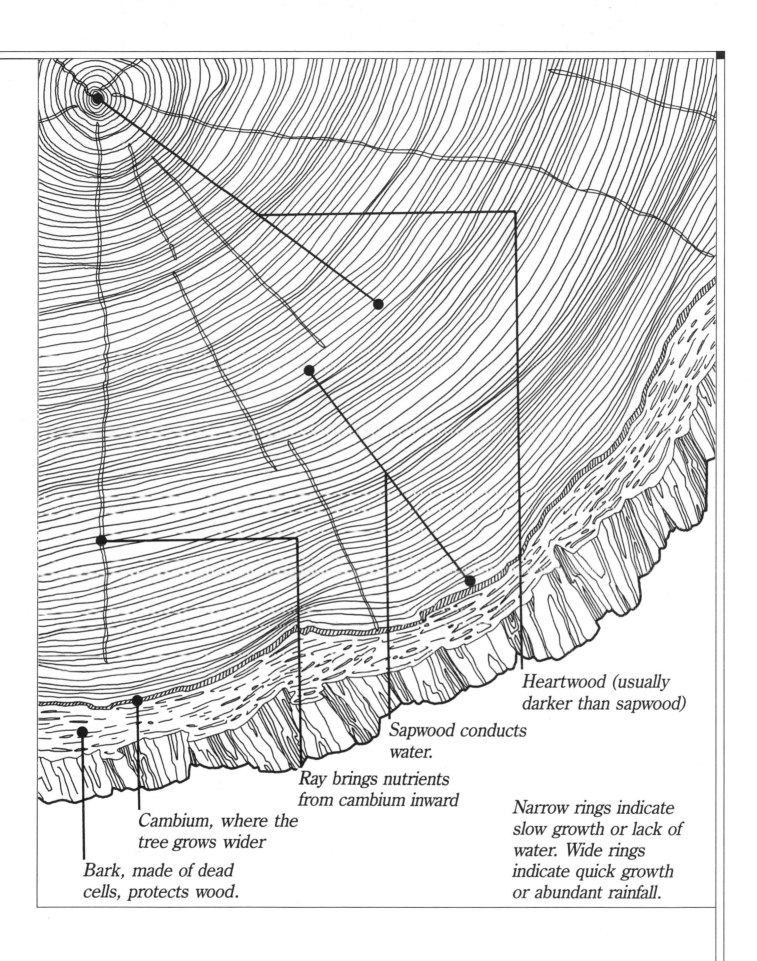

Heartwood (usually darker than sapwood)

Sapwood conducts water.

Ray brings nutrients from cambium inward

Cambium, where the tree grows wider

Bark, made of dead cells, protects wood.

Narrow rings indicate slow growth or lack of water. Wide rings indicate quick growth or abundant rainfall.

PART THREE
NORTH AMERICAN
FORESTS

The Oldest Living Trees

The oldest tree alive lives on a rocky slope high in the White Mountains of California. It sprouted there more than 4,500 years ago, while the pyramids of Egypt were being built. It's been 45 centuries since then, and the tree is still putting out new shoots. No one knows how much longer it might live.

That tree, and other bristlecone pines, live in places where most plants could not grow well. For one thing, they grow on mountains about 10,000 feet high—so high that some people would have a hard time breathing there. On these mountainsides the soil is very shallow, and there is only about 10 inches of rainfall a year. The winter months are very cold, and summer is very hot and dry. It's a harsh environment where hardly anything can grow. Twisted and gnarled, bristlecone pines look as though they have been tortured by this harsh environment. But these trees seem to thrive in such harsh conditions.

When you picture a thriving tree, you probably picture a lot of greenery. The older bristlecone pines don't fit the picture. In fact, from a distance, they look dead. Focus on one and it appears to be nothing but a stump. Move closer, and you'll see that part of the trunk is dead, its wood turned shiny and white like a piece of driftwood that you might find by the ocean. This dead wood continues to stand upright, often for hundreds of years, while other parts of the tree continue to grow.

The living parts of the tree bear short green needles and cones that carry the seeds of the future trees. Each scale of a female cone has a bristle at its end—and that, of course, is why these trees are called bristlecone pines.

Bristlecone pines

48

The Tallest Trees

On the foggy coast of northern California lives the tallest tree in the world, a redwood tree more than 360 feet tall. It lives in a forest of redwoods, climbing only a little higher into the sky than many of its neighbors.

It's hard to picture trees that tall, but try this: that's taller than a football field is long!

Redwoods have thick trunks, too. One redwood tree, known as the Dyerville Giant, has a trunk 52 feet around. To get some idea how big that is, measure the span of your arms, from one set of fingertips to the other (let's say the distance is four feet). Then divide that number (4) into 52. Now you know how many friends your size you would need to make a circle the size of the Dyerville Giant's trunk. If each kid's arm span were four feet, you'd need yourself plus a dozen friends to form the circle. Think how many people could sit cross-legged inside the circle. That Dyerville Giant is a very big tree!

Redwoods once covered a couple of million acres along the coasts of California and Oregon, thriving in the frequent ocean fogs that blanketed them there. As more and more people moved to this beautiful area, large areas of forest were cut to make room for houses. Redwood timber is prized as lumber, and many, many of these trees have been cut down for their wood. Fortunately, redwoods are such beautiful trees that people wanted to preserve them. Now many parks are dedicated to keeping redwood forests for everyone to enjoy.

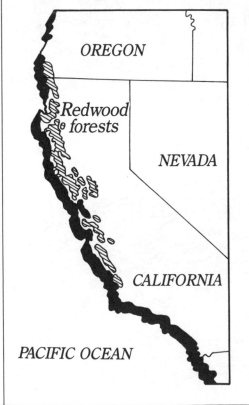

A Northern Rain Forest

If we were to hike up the West Coast, beyond the home of the redwoods, we'd come to something surprising—a northern rain forest!

Olympic National Park, in the state of Washington, is a northern rain forest. It gets about 145 inches of rain a year. Like a redwood forest, it also gets a lot of fog. Hikers there are almost always damp!

Trees that grow in a northern rain forest are different from those that grow in a tropical rain forest, but they can grow just as tall. Sitka spruce trees, which are found in Olympic National Park, may grow nearly 200 feet tall—as tall as a 20-story building.

The Sitka spruce is a cone-bearing tree, sometimes called an evergreen because its needle-like leaves stay green all year round. Other evergreens grow in this northern rain forest, too. Growing alongside the evergreens are some trees with broad leaves that fall off in the autumn.

Because a northern rain forest gets so much rain and fog, two special kinds of plants can grow there. One kind is a plant that needs no soil. It is called an air plant, or epiphyte (see page 30). Instead of putting roots into the soil to support itself, it uses another plant for support. The second kind is called moss. Moss often covers fallen logs and the exposed roots of trees. Mosses are simple plants with no veins in their stems to move water and food up and down. So, all parts of a moss plant need almost constant moisture.

Unlike hikers, who want dry clothes at the end of the day, epiphytes and mosses like to be damp!

Sitka spruce

A Northern Conifer Forest

The call of the common loon is the cry of the wilderness, a sound that once heard is never forgotten. In the United States, this handsome bird of the north nests along the shores of quiet lakes from Minnesota to Maine. Many of these lakes are bordered by evergreen forests that are dominated by cone-bearing trees known as *conifers*. (Conifer means cone-bearing.) Most of the cone-bearing trees in these forests are spruce, pine, hemlock, or fir—all trees with needle-like leaves that stay green all winter.

Loons and many other animals live in these quiet evergreen forests, where they can raise their young unbothered by humans or speeding boats. Forest parks are perfect places, offering protection, privacy, and lots of small lakes.

If you were to go to Maine and visit a lake in Baxter State Park, you might hear a loon calling to its mate. If you were lucky, you might even see a loon swimming along the surface. But not for long! Pretty soon, the loon would disappear under the water, diving in search of a fish for its dinner. The common loon is also called "great northern diver."

Another animal that lives in the northern forests is the huge, stately moose. These members of the deer family are much larger than their relatives, growing to be 7½ feet tall at the shoulder and weighing up to 1,800 pounds. The male moose has antlers that may spread six feet wide.

The same lake that provides fish for the loons provides water plants for the moose, which graze along the shoreline and wade in the shallow water to feed on plants.

ANIMAL TRACKER

The moose is the largest mammal with branched antlers.

Moose live in the northern forests of North America and in northern Europe, where they are usually called elk.

Moose have long legs and broad hooves that let them walk easily through marshy terrain. They like to eat plants that grow in water, and they are good swimmers.

Moose

The Sugar Bush

When European settlers came to New England in the early 1600s, they soon discovered the sugar maple tree. It was an important discovery because the tree gave them many things they needed. Its wood is hard and can be polished to a lovely reddish-brown shine—perfect for furniture and floors. In a fireplace, sugar maple burns slowly, making it an efficient source of heat. Settlers used the ashes to make soap.

Sugar maple trees made the settlers' hard lives a little easier, and a lot sweeter. The sap of this tree is the source of maple syrup.

Other maples—the black, the silver, and the red—can be used to make syrup, but the sugar maple is the biggest producer. Each year, about 40 gallons of sap can be collected from a single tree. But 40 gallons of sap doesn't make 40 gallons of syrup.

Raw sap is very watery and must be boiled and boiled until most of the water evaporates as steam. When the boiling is done, that 40 gallons of sap has made only one gallon of syrup! To make more concentrated sap products, such as maple cream or maple sugar candy, even the little water left in the syrup must be boiled away.

Sap starts flowing inside a sugar maple tree in late winter or early spring, when the days begin to grow warm and sunny. A farmer or sap collector uses a special tool to bore a small hole about three inches into the trunk and then inserts a hollow tap, through which the sap drips into a bucket or bag hung underneath it.

Sugar maple forests, known as the sugar bush, grow mostly in eastern Canada and the northern and eastern United States. This useful tree is also beautiful, growing up to 135 feet high and spreading its branches wide enough to shade a large picnic spot.

The Pine Barrens

Fire! Forest fire!

These words frighten us all, especially if we have ever seen a blaze spreading out of control. Some forests, however, have always known fires, and the plants that grow in them manage very well. One such forest is the Pine Barrens of southern New Jersey, located not far from the cities of New York and Philadelphia.

It seems odd that the word "barren" would be used to name a forest, because "barren" usually describes a place where nothing will grow. In the Pine Barrens, one thing grows very well: the pitch pine tree, a smallish, cone-bearing evergreen.

The soil in this unusual forest is very sandy, so rain drains through it quickly. On the ground are many small twigs and dead needles dropped from the pitch pines. When this plant debris dries—as it does quickly atop such sandy soil—it catches fire easily.

A fire can start from lightning or from human carelessness: a burning cigarette tossed aside, campfire coals no one remembered to smother. Once fire starts, it spreads rapidly. Scientists think that fires used to happen naturally in the Pine Barrens every 20 years or so.

The pitch pine has three ways to cope with fire. First, it has a thick, fire-resistant bark. A swiftly moving fire won't harm it. Second, it has a secret store of buds hidden under its thick bark. After a fire, the buds sprout, and soon the tree has new needles to replace ones burned away by fire.

Third, some cones stay tightly closed until there is a fire. The intense heat causes these cones to open. Their seeds then drift out and land on soil that has been cleared of debris by the fire. Almost immediately, these seeds begin to grow—far sooner than any other tree nearby.

If fires that start naturally in the Pine Barrens were put out too quickly, the natural balance of life there would change. To maintain that balance, fires are needed. But wildfires can be very dangerous. So foresters protect the Pine Barrens by starting small fires they are trained to control. Foresters who start forest fires: Isn't that an unusual way to protect a forest?

Holly Forests

To see a redwood forest, you have to go to the West Coast, to the environment of fog and rain where these trees thrive. Several other kinds of forests need certain conditions to develop fully. The holly forests on the East Coast of the United States are a good example. You probably have seen sprigs or wreaths of holly at Christmastime. American holly is an evergreen with thick, shiny, spiny leaves. For much of the year, it has bright red fruits—a very festive plant all year round.

American holly grows from Massachusetts to Texas, usually alongside other trees. In a few places, such as Fire Island, New York, and Sandy Hook, New Jersey, there are more holly trees than any other kind of tree.

Why does American holly do so well in these places? Fire Island and Sandy Hook both have very sandy soil, and the trees that grow there are exposed to salt spray blown in from the ocean. Lots of other plants do well in sandy soil, but would be killed by salt spray. Holly grows well in sand and is not bothered by salt. Fire Island and Sandy Hook are just right for holly, and wrong for maples, elms, and other trees that might otherwise compete for space to grow.

These holly forests are not large, but they are important to birds and mammals. Holly berries are a good source of food for many birds and small animals during winter. A bird may swallow a berry whole; mice and other small rodents nibble the fruits open and eat the seeds inside. They are all gaining energy to help them through the long winter.

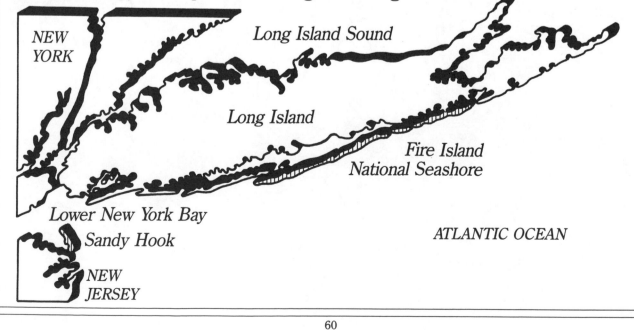

NEW YORK

Long Island Sound

Long Island

Fire Island National Seashore

Lower New York Bay

Sandy Hook

NEW JERSEY

ATLANTIC OCEAN

A Live Oak Forest

Some of the most beautiful forests in the United States are oak forests—the live oak forests that thrive along the southeastern coast, in South Carolina, Georgia, and northern Florida.

Why do you suppose one kind of oak tree is called a live oak when it is no more alive than any other kind of oak? If you've ever seen a live oak in the winter, you know.

A live oak tree is very unusual. Other oaks lose their leaves in the autumn and are bare until spring. A live oak keeps its leaves all winter long, until a new set of leaves emerges to take their place. When other oak trees look dead, it looks alive. (If your science teacher asks you whether oak trees are deciduous, you can answer "Not all of them!")

The leaves of a live oak are oval, not lobed like many other oak leaves. A live oak, like all oaks, begins to bear acorns when it matures, a process that takes about 20 years.

Live oaks are tall and have spreading branches, so they are also very wide. They grow especially well on sandy soil protected from the ocean by wide beaches and sand dunes. Spanish moss often hangs from their spreading branches. The forest floor beneath is smooth and soft, and the sound of the not-so-distant ocean is ever-present. Walking among these trees is like being in an enchanted forest.

In the Shelter of the Bald Cypress

This mother alligator, with her babies riding safely on her back, is enjoying the food she finds in the waters of a cypress swamp—*lots* of fish. Fish of many sizes live in these waters, and the alligator is just one of the creatures that depend on these fish.

Big wading birds gather around open water areas, especially during the winter, when the southern United States receives little rain. At night they roost in the safety of bald cypress trees. By day they stand patiently waiting in the water, as motionless as if they were carved from stone—until a fish comes too close. Then, almost faster than we can see, the birds strike, spearing fish with their beaks, swallowing, and becoming motionless once again.

Most wading birds, and most smaller birds that also winter in Florida, migrate north when spring comes. One bird that stays is the wood stork, which builds big nests high in the protection of bald cypress trees.

The wood stork is the only true stork found in all of North America, and a cypress swamp is the best place to go to see one. As if alligators weren't reason enough!

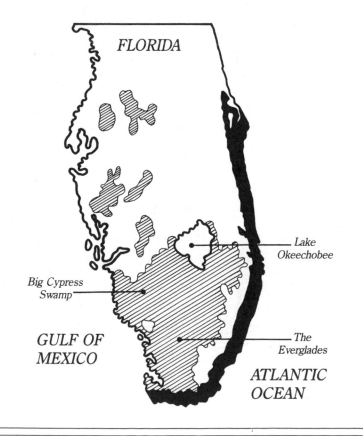

FLORIDA

Lake Okeechobee

Big Cypress Swamp

GULF OF MEXICO

The Everglades

ATLANTIC OCEAN

A Mangrove Forest

It is dawn in a mangrove forest.

The sun's first rays light up the quiet tidal flat. Only a few inches deep, the salt waters of this vast area support a great variety of fish, crabs, snails, and animals too small for us to see.

Wading birds that have roosted in the mangrove trees overnight are waking up hungry. In the shallow water below, they begin to see the swarming shapes of fish and crabs moving over and around snails and other ocean creatures.

Now they fly down to feed on the teeming life beneath the water's surface. Roseate spoonbills, like a streaming pink banner hurled against the dawn's pale sky, follow one another down to breakfast. They are joined by ibises, and many kinds of herons that have sheltered in the same trees.

These trees are part of what many people consider one of the most interesting and important forests of all—the mangrove forest. Most of North America's mangroves are in southern Florida.

Mangrove is the name given to several species of tree that can grow in or very near salt water. Most land plants cannot live in salt water.

In our part of the world, there are three common kinds of mangrove plants (there are 55 species worldwide). Our three are called red, white, and black mangrove. They don't look much alike, but they are always found in the same places, along the shores of subtropical and tropical coasts all over the world.

BEAK BOX

Water birds have interesting beaks.

The roseate spoonbill swings its flattened bill from side to side, snapping down on any food it finds.

The white ibis rakes the muddy swamp bottom with its feet to catch small animals in its bill.

The pelican dives into the ocean to catch fish, which it holds in its pouch before swallowing them.

The Red Mangrove

One kind of mangrove is so unusual that it's hard to believe—the red mangrove. This tree grows right in the salt water, nearer the ocean than any other mangrove tree.

There it develops a great tangle of roots that curve down from the tree trunks into the water. All the roots of all the trees growing together form an interlocking network. Raccoons can scamper along the tops of these roots, looking for oysters and other shellfish that live on them, but you and I would never be able to move quickly or easily through this barricade.

Fallen leaves and other plants get caught in this tangle of roots. They sink to the bottom and decay, releasing nutrients that feed tiny plants and animals which live in the water. Eventually, as this plant debris accumulates, new soil forms beneath the roots. So, over time, the mangrove actually adds land to the shoreline.

The red mangrove does one more truly unusual thing. It bears fruit with a seed inside, just as an apple grows. Apples fall off the tree when they are ripe, but not a red mangrove fruit. While a mangrove fruit is still on the tree, a root begins to grow from it, and a mangrove fruit can grow two or more feet toward the water while still attached to the tree! Then the whole fruit falls in the water and drifts along to a shallow place where it takes root and grows into another red mangrove tree. Quite a trick!

Kelp

When you think of seaweed, you probably don't think of forests. But if you could walk along the bottom of the ocean, somewhere off the coast of northern California, into an area where giant kelp grows, you would describe that area as an underwater forest.

Kelp is a brown seaweed, and giant kelp is the largest seaweed in the world. Some kelp grows more than 300 feet long—the height of a good-sized redwood tree.

A giant kelp is not a tree, of course. (Although a few kinds of trees grow in water, no tree grows underwater.) But a giant kelp looks something like a tree. It has a thick stem with leaf-like blades growing along it. A root-like structure called a holdfast is at the base of the stem, holding the kelp to rocks on the ocean floor. As the ocean water moves, the giant kelp sways with it, just as trees sway in the wind.

A community of giant kelp is called a forest because so many of these large plants grow so close together over large areas. A human swimmer would seem tiny in comparison to these plants and the areas that they cover.

Just as many animals are part of a forest on land, many animals are part of the giant kelp forest, too. Sea otters live in this forest, diving down into the water to collect their food. A favorite food item is the abalone, a kind of snail that holds tightly onto rocks on the ocean floor.

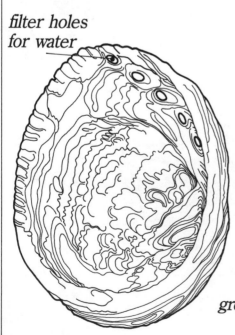

filter holes for water

A sea otter, which looks somewhat like a seal, so loves to eat abalone that it will work very hard to get some. It must dive down deep to find one, and then pry it off its rock. Once the otter has this prize, it clasps the abalone to its belly and floats upward through the giant kelp to the surface. There, while floating on its back, the otter uses a rock to smash the abalone shell and enjoy the fleshy abalone meat inside.

green abalone

Sea otters eat abalone.

PART FOUR

FORESTS FROM THE NORTH POLE TO THE SOUTH

The Taiga

Forests can grow in places where the weather is very hot, and in places where the weather is very cold. But they cannot grow where there is too little water.

Near the North Pole, there is lots of water, but it is always frozen and so it is useless to plants. If you were to go to the North Pole and travel south, you would cover many miles of snow and ice before you saw any plants. Only when you reach an area called the tundra do temperatures rise enough to melt the snow for a few weeks a year. Lichens and mosses thrive in the tundra, but little else.

ANIMAL TRACKER

Female reindeer and caribou have something that no other female deer have—antlers! (Of course, male reindeer and caribou also have antlers.)

Reindeer may be from 2½ to 4½ feet tall at the shoulder. They have long front legs and broad hooves that they spread to wade through marshes or to walk in deep snow.

When they travel from their summer pastures to their winter pastures, reindeer travel in big herds.

You would have to travel south a few hundred miles more before you would find the tree line, at the northern edge of the world's northernmost forests. These forests are called the *taiga* (TIE-gah). They are forests of mostly cone-bearing trees that border the tundra, stretching in an uneven belt around the top of the world.

A taiga is a swampy forest, with many lakes and bogs scattered through it. The trees—mostly spruces, cedars, firs, and pines—grow spaced widely apart. Compared with the dense spruce forests of the northern United States, these trees seem very scattered indeed.

The best-known animals of this forest are reindeer: known in North America as caribou. For generations, people in northern Europe have herded reindeer, much in the same way that people in our country herd cattle. They eat reindeer meat, drink reindeer milk, and make leather from reindeer hides.

A herd of reindeer

The Black Forest

Most children know the scary story of Hansel and Gretel. You may know that it's an old German folk tale. But you may not know that the dark woods where Hansel and Gretel come upon the gingerbread house is very much like a real forest, the Black Forest of southwestern West Germany.

The woods of that region have captured the imagination of many storytellers. It is a region of steep, rugged mountains bordering the Rhine River valley. It gets its name from the fir trees that blanket the upper slopes of the mountainsides. The trees are so dark a shade of green, they look almost black.

The trees of the Black Forest are an excellent source of lumber, so valued that new trees are planted whenever old ones are cut. Craftsmen of the region use the wood to make cuckoo clocks that are sold all over the world.

The Black Forest offers tourists and vacationers a rare combination of natural attractions. Miles and miles of scenic trails lure hikers in the summer. Snowy slopes lure skiers in the winter. Health spas have sprung up around the many mineral springs in this region, where people go to drink mineral water and refresh themselves by bathing in the pure waters of the springs. Nature-lovers come to enjoy the plants and animals in their unspoiled setting.

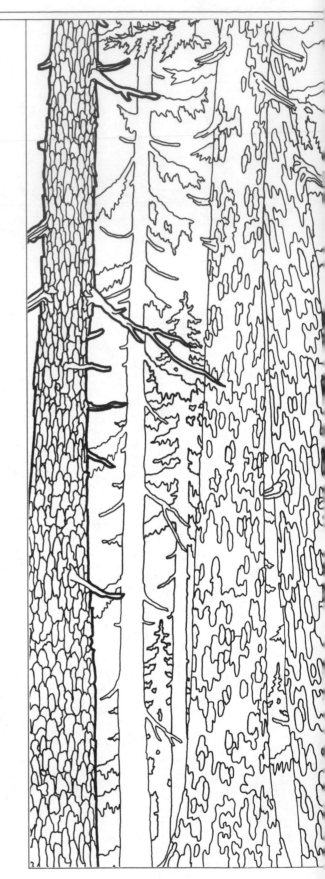

China's Bamboo Forests

Can you think of a bear-like animal that's black and white, very big, and very, very rare? The only animal that fits the description is the giant panda, and the only place to find a giant panda (outside a zoo) is in the bamboo forests high in the mountains of central China.

Like many other rare animals, the giant panda is rare because it can live in only one place. That place is a mountain region 10,000 feet above sea level, where several kinds of bamboo grow in dense thickets.

Bamboo provides shelter for pandas, which hide so well in the thickets they are nearly impossible to find. Scientists who want to study wild pandas must bait a trap with meat and wait.

Giant pandas *are among the world's most beautiful and rare creatures. When fully grown, they can be nearly five feet long and weigh 200 pounds.*

Pandas eat bamboo. They have a special "thumb" bone in their wrists that helps them to grasp bamboo stalks.

Not many of these animals are left in the world, and the future of the giant panda is uncertain. Scientists are trying to breed pandas in zoos, and China has set aside 12 large areas to protect them.

Bamboo provides pandas with almost all of their food. The ancestors of present-day pandas were meat-eaters, and a panda will gladly eat meat if it is offered, but will not hunt for it. Instead, a panda eats what is readily available: the shoots, leaves, and stems of bamboo plants.

Bamboo may grow 120 feet tall, with a stem as much as a foot across, but it is not a tree. It is related to wheat, oats, and barley.

To get enough to eat, a panda must eat about 40 pounds of bamboo a day. That's a lot of bamboo, and it's not surprising that each panda needs a lot of bamboo forest to live in.

continued on page 82

Giant pandas eat bamboo.

China's Bamboo Forests, *continued*

China has established more than a dozen nature reserves to help preserve the panda and the bamboo it needs. The most famous of these reserves, Wulong, covers 770 square miles, an area about half the size of the state of Rhode Island. There research is being done on pandas and on bamboo by international teams of scientists.

This research is important because there are probably only about a thousand pandas left in the wild, and we need to know about them in order to know best how to save them.

We already know that cutting down forests has destroyed a lot of bamboo forest where pandas used to live. That's one reason the Chinese decided to create so many nature reserves. They want to protect the bamboo forest that still remains, so that there will always be forests where pandas can live.

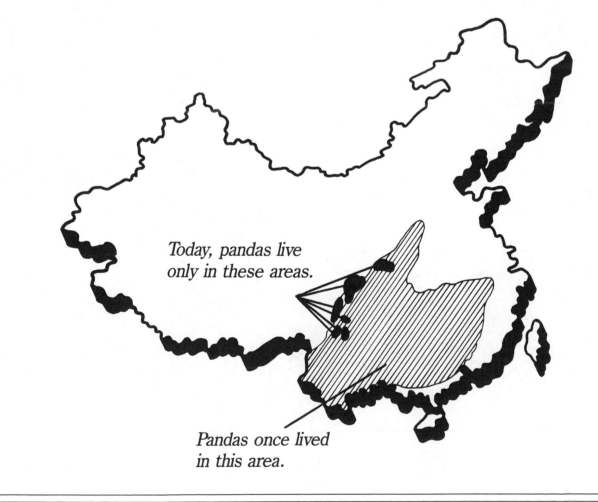

Today, pandas live only in these areas.

Pandas once lived in this area.

A Living Fossil

In a hidden valley, deep in the interior of China, is a small forest with an amazing story. It is the only known forest of a tree called the dawn redwood, or *Metasequoia* (met-a-seh-KOY-a).

This forest was not discovered by scientists until 1941. Before that, scientists had found only fossil remains of the dawn redwood. They thought it was extinct!

A dawn redwood tree looks very much like the bald cypress trees that grow in the southeastern United States. But, perhaps because it does not often live in a swamp as a bald cypress does, a dawn redwood does not usually have the "knees" that identify a bald cypress.

When a Chinese scientist discovered the dawn redwood forest, word spread quickly to scientists around the world. They were thrilled to hear of a "living fossil"! It is difficult to travel to the remote area where the dawn redwood lives, but within a few years after its discovery, several scientists from the United States made the long trip to collect seeds for study.

The Chinese consider the dawn redwood a national treasure. The forest is protected by the government of China just as some forests in the United States are protected by the National Park system.

Chinese scientists have counted 5,240 trees in the forest. None of these trees may be cut down or harmed in any way. Scientists say that the trees seem very healthy, so we can hope that they will all be preserved for future generations to enjoy.

China's Metasequoia forest

Rhododendrons

Among the flowering shrubs you see in parks and gardens every spring, one stands out. It is taller and wider than the rest, and boasts the biggest clumps of flowers—purest white, deepest red, and every shade of pink in between. It is the rhododendron.

There are many kinds, some the size of an average bush, and some the size of a tree: 40 feet tall and nearly as wide. Popular as an ornamental plant in Europe and North America, the rhododendron is often planted in small, private gardens and along the walkways of large public parks. It also grows wild in many parts of North America and Europe.

In an isolated part of central Asia, rhododendrons cover the lower slopes of the world's highest mountains in forests stretching as far as the eye can see. The place is Nepal, the small nation between northern India and the plateau of Tibet in western China.

Much of Nepal is made up of the Himalayas, the mountain range where Mt. Everest reaches more than 29,000 feet into the clouds. The tops of the mountains are covered with snow all year. Between the peaks and their bases, the climate varies.

At an altitude of 8,000 to 10,000 feet, these mountains get more rain than some rain forests. The weather is cool, moist, and often foggy. That's perfect for rhododendrons—they grow so thickly in some places that it is impossible to walk among them.

All year, the evergreen rhododendron lends its glossy, dark-green beauty to the Himalayas. In spring it bursts into glorious color. To stand on a hillside facing the mountain slopes, to see the blossoms framed by the snow-covered mountain peaks and a clear mountain sky, will take your breath away.

Map showing the Himalayan Mountains, Plateau of Tibet, CHINA, NEPAL, Mt. Everest, BHUTAN, INDIA, BANGLADESH, and a forest region.

The African Forest

When you think of the things that make Africa special, you probably think of its animals. Many of the most popular animals at any zoo are African animals: the lion, the leopard, the monkey, and, of course, the majestic African elephant, the largest land mammal of them all.

Africa is rich in animal life partly because it has so many different combinations of weather and terrain where animals can live. There are vast deserts in northern Africa, tropical rain forests in the Congo River basin, and between them, wide-open tropical grasslands.

Most often when we see pictures of elephants, they are roaming in family herds across the grasslands. But elephants also live in forests—not rain forests, but forests that fringe the grasslands. In these woodlands, rainfall is moderate and the seasons alternate from wet to dry. Like forests everywhere, they provide shelter and food for animals.

continued on page 90

The African Forest, *continued*

The African elephant eats mostly grass. In one year, one animal eats a pile of grass the size of a good sledding hill. But elephants also eat trees. They use their ivory tusks to scrape off the bark, dig up roots, or pry open the trunks of trees to get at the soft wood inside.

African forests are home to a host of other splendid and fascinating animals. Lions sometimes lie stretched along the branches of trees, waiting for unsuspecting prey to walk beneath them.

Leopards chase their food in open areas, but when they are successful they will carry their captured dinner up into trees, beyond the reach of hyenas that would like to share the meal without doing any of the work!

Monkeys, of course, live in African forests. Many monkeys use their long tails to swing from branch to branch high above the forest floor.

Sharing the African woodlands with such creatures as elephants, lions, leopards, and monkeys, are many smaller animals that are just as interesting. Butterflies drifting among the trees make the forest a kaleidoscope of ever-changing colors, as they go from one exotic flower to another. Tree frogs sit still against their leafy backgrounds, as caterpillars munch upon the leaves around them. Birds unlike any we are used to seeing search for food, build their nests, and raise their young.

ANIMAL TRACKER

Leopards move so quietly that they often can surprise their prey. They live alone, and do most of their hunting at dusk or after dark. The leopard is smaller than a lion or tiger, and slower than a cheetah, but this big cat is a very good hunter. Once it has caught an animal, a leopard often drags its prey into a tree to keep it safe from other hungry meat-eating animals.

Leopards live in much of Asia and in Africa, except the deserts.

African leopard

Tropical Rain Forests

Tropical rain forests are warm, wet, and wondrous! They cover only about seven percent of the land on Earth, but scientists think that half the plants and animals that can be found anywhere on land can be found in tropical rain forests.

Tropical rain forests form a wide belt around the widest part of the globe, the equator. This is the region of the world that is hot, humid, and rainy just about all year long.

Colombia, a South American country right on the equator, sometimes receives 400 inches of rain in one year. If you wanted to collect that much rain in a pool, your pool would have to be more than 33 feet deep!

Rain forests grow where it rains almost every day, and the humidity is so high that plants stay moist even when it isn't raining. Growing conditions in the tropics are so good for so many kinds of plants that there is a struggle for life-giving sunlight. Plants climb on, around, over, and up other plants.

As a result of all this lush growth, some parts of the forest floor are dark even during the day. That doesn't bother the animals that live in these forests. Many of them are creatures of the night, sleeping during steamy days and rousing to forage or hunt when the sun goes down.

continued on page 94

Tropical Rain Forests, *continued*

Any study of animal life in a rain forest is very difficult. But if you could camp out in one South American rain forest (and survive the insects!), you would glimpse the incredible variety of animal life to be found in these areas.

There are toucans, birds with colorful bills that seem much too large for their bodies. There are leaf-cutter ants that form seemingly endless lines, each ant carrying a piece of a leaf on its back. Monkeys howl from high above the forest floor. Snakes stretch sleepily along tree limbs, and sluggish sloths hang upside down, apparently never doing anything at all! Flowers glow like jewels in the shadowed depths, and colorful butterflies soar to and fro.

It's quite a place!

ANIMAL TRACKER

Sloths live in trees, *and almost never climb down to the ground. They cannot walk easily; instead, they usually pull themselves along with their claws. Their paws are curved, with long claws that help them cling to tree trunks and hang upside-down from branches.*

There are two types of sloths: three-toed, including the maned sloth shown here; and two-toed. All sloths are gentle, leaf-eating animals which move so slowly that very small, single-celled plants sometimes grow on their fur.

Forests of Ferns

One of the most beautiful forests has no trees—it's made of gigantic ferns.

Growing conditions in the warm, wet tropics are so good that many kinds of plants grow very large. Some are so large, and have such tough, stiff stems, that they are often mistaken for trees.

Such a plant is the tree fern. Its first name tells you what it looks like. Its last name tells you what it is.

Like the lacy ferns you might see growing a foot or two tall in a North American forest, a tree fern is descended from ferns that first grew hundreds of millions of years ago, before there were any real trees.

A tree fern's slender stem is strong and wood-like, but it's not made of wood, like the trunk of a tree. A fern's stems do, however, function the way a tree's trunk functions. Veins inside the stems carry water from the roots to the leaves, and carry food made by the leaves to other parts of the plant.

The plants that we call trees all have seeds, either in cones or in fruits. Ferns have no seeds. Instead, they have spores, usually on the undersides of the leaves. Lift up any fern leaf and you may see little brown dots in rows along its length. Each dot contains many, many spores. Like seeds, spores can develop into new plants. They're very small, but each spore of a tropical tree fern may someday sprout into a plant taller than a four-story building!

Insect-eating Plants

A *very* unusual plant can be found in the humid rain forests of Malaysia, a small country barely above the equator in southeast Asia.

The rain forests of Malaysia are home to the giant pitcher plant, a plant that eats insects. This is not the only insect-eating plant in the world—in fact, there are several such plants in the United States—but it sets the most ingenious trap.

The giant pitcher plant grows as a vine among the rain forest trees. Its leaves are shaped like a lovely pitcher that you might use to pour water. But this pitcher has one purpose: to trap insects.

Look inside the pitcher and you will see how it's done. The bright red rim is lined with downward-pointing spikes. Just below the rim, the leaves have glands that secrete chemicals attractive to insects. Once an insect has crawled or flown to the rim, it slides down the spikes to the bottom of the pitcher. The inside of the pitcher plant is so smooth and waxy that the insect cannot climb out past the spikes. At the bottom of the pitcher is a pool of liquid that the leaf has secreted, and this liquid contains complex substances that will digest the trapped insect.

To keep its digestive fluids from being watered down by the frequent rains, each leaf of the pitcher plant has a heart-shaped cap that acts as an umbrella. Amazing!

Scientists know that insect-eating plants often grow in boggy soil which is very low in a nutrient called nitrogen. They think that when a plant digests an insect, it uses nitrogen from the insect's body to build up its own supply.

CHINA

PHILIPPINE SEA

MALAYSIA

Pitcher plants

The World's Largest Flower

Tremendous trees are often the forest plants that catch and hold our attention. Every forest, however, also has interesting smaller plants, and some of these are truly astonishing.

Consider, for example, a plant found in the rain forests of Malaysia, far on the other side of the world. This plant is called *Rafflesia* (raf-FLEES-ee-uh), and it has the biggest flowers of any plant in the world.

These flowers, with rust-orange centers and five brown petals as thick as shoe leather, can be as much as three feet wide. That may be as wide as you (or your younger sister or brother) are tall!

In fact, if you got a big piece of brown paper and drew a three-foot-wide outline like this:

I think you'd find you could sit cross-legged on it and not go over the edge. (You could color it and have a rafflesia-rug!)

Rafflesia has other surprises. Unlike most plants, this huge flower is a parasite. That means it doesn't produce its own food, but depends on a host plant for its survival. Rafflesia lives on a vine and takes from it the materials that it needs in order to grow.

Because it depends on other plants for its food, rafflesia doesn't need any green tissue of its own. Its very tiny leaves and stem grow at the base of the huge flower. The flower has to be carefully cut away in order to even see them.

rafflesia flower

Southern Beech Forests

Millions of years ago, the earth's land masses were very different from today. In the southern part of the world was a supercontinent that has since split into several smaller continents.

Part of this supercontinent was covered by dense forests of southern beech. When the land broke up and new, smaller land masses spread apart over the earth's surface, beech forests went along.

Today, the earth looks very different from the way it did millions of years ago, but present-day southern beech forests look very much like ancient ones.

Southern beech can be found in places as far apart as New Zealand and southern South America. Fossils of these trees have even been found deep beneath Antarctic ice!

Because there is a lot of rain in places where these beech forests grow, mosses are everywhere. They cover branches, trunks, fallen logs, and even leaves with a dense, luxuriant blanket, giving the forest a mysterious appearance.

In addition to this thick, soft layer of moss are dozens of kinds of ferns. They grow right on the beech trees, dripping down from every branch, and adding to the enchanted atmosphere.

These vast, cathedral-like forests are quiet, save for the occasional call of some exotic bird. Far from civilization, these forests may be as close to a truly primeval forest as any on earth.

135 million years ago   *65 million years ago*

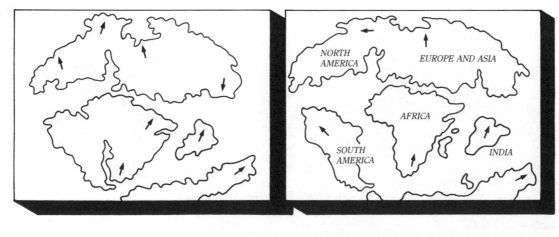

Gum Trees

"Kookaburra sits on the old gum tree...."

Familiar words from a familiar song, but whatever do they mean?

The kookaburra is a bird—a giant kingfisher. Gum tree is another name for Australia's most common forest tree, the eucalyptus (you-kuh-LIP-tus). Nearly 500 kinds of eucalyptus are native to Australia. They grow very well in other countries that have the right climate, but they evolved in Australia.

In this country we've all heard about kangaroos and koalas. We know that they are special Australian animals, but not everyone realizes that Australia has special trees, too. Some eucalyptus trees can grow nearly as tall as redwoods, the world's tallest trees. Most eucalyptus trees are evergreen. Their leaves are an unusual blueish-green color, slender and pointed. An oil in their leaves has a strong, distinctive, and quite pleasant odor.

Since eucalyptus are the most common trees in Australia, it's not surprising that Australians have found many uses for them. Here are some: medicine, perfume, honey, timber, tannin, animal food, railroad ties, plywood, shade trees, paper pulp, dance floors, furniture, and deodorants. Don't these sound like useful trees?

They are useful to humans, and they are even more useful to one Australian animal—can you guess which one?

Koalas

The koala is an Australian animal that needs eucalyptus trees to survive. These animals that we find so appealing spend their entire lives in eucalyptus forests.

Like kangaroos, baby koalas spend the first few months of their lives living in a pouch on their mother's abdomen.

Koala families spend their days in the safety of eucalyptus treetops. There they rest and sleep until dinner time and the dark of night, when they are most active.

The only food koalas can eat is the fully grown leaves of about half a dozen kinds of eucalyptus, or gum trees. An adult koala eats about two and a half pounds of leaves every day! The leaves provide all the nourishment and all the moisture a koala needs.

Without gum trees, there would be no koalas, and the world would be a little less wonderful. Doesn't it make you wonder what treasures are lost when unexplored forests are destroyed? What plants and animals might disappear without our ever having known they existed?

We're lucky to know about koalas!

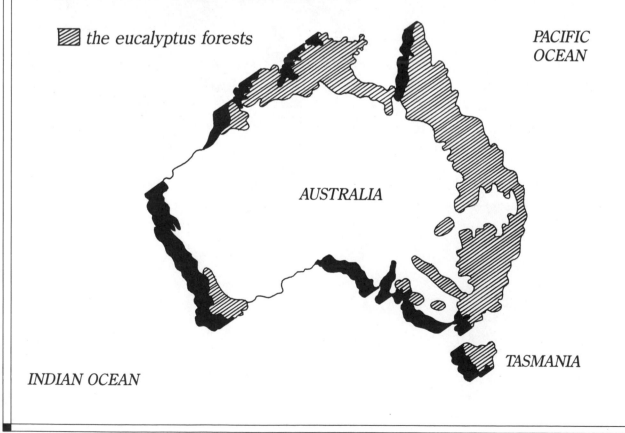

the eucalyptus forests

PACIFIC OCEAN

AUSTRALIA

TASMANIA

INDIAN OCEAN

PART FIVE
FORESTS FOR THE FUTURE

Forests Serve Many Needs

As you've "leafed" through this book, reading about some of the world's forests, you may have decided that forests should be saved for the simple reason that they are beautiful and interesting.

What do we say to someone who doesn't feel the way we do? Lots of people see forests as places to be cleared for houses. Others think pasture for cattle is more important than trees for monkeys to live in. These people think that other things are more important than forests.

Are there reasons to save forests that go beyond their beauty and interest? *Of course there are!*

For one truly excellent example let's go to Madagascar. This island lies east of Africa, and was joined to it many millions of years ago. Since it became an island, plants and animals have evolved there that are known nowhere else in the world.

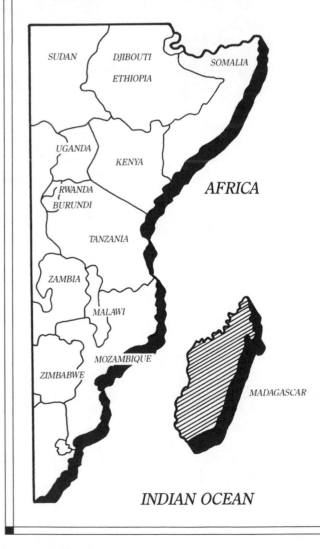

One plant on this island has a very important medicinal use. Called the Madagascar periwinkle, this flower looks rather like a periwinkle that you might have in your garden. Chemicals from it are used to fight childhood leukemia—a dreadful blood disease that once was thought to have no cure. This plant is helping to save lives.

This periwinkle is not a plant of the deep forests, but a related and far rarer kind of flower does grow there. Who knows what use *it* might have one day?

Protecting Forests from Disease

Fossils show us that some trees that once were alive no longer exist. When the last plant or animal of its kind dies, we say that it is extinct. In the present, as people cut down whole forests for lumber, for cattle grazing, or for development, there is a growing concern that many plants and animals now alive also will become extinct.

We know that it is possible for a rare tree to become extinct in the wild in modern times (see the amazing story on page 118). The story of the American chestnut warns us that even common trees are at risk.

This magnificent tree once covered thousands and thousands of acres in the southern Appalachian Mountains. It towered over the early settlers who sought a living on these forested slopes. Who would have thought that trees so huge and so common could ever be in danger?

Around 1900, a fungus was brought into the United States by accident on an Asian chestnut tree. This fungus attacked the American chestnut trees, spreading quickly from one forest to the next. By the 1950s, all fully grown American chestnut trees had died. Sometimes shoots still grow from old stumps, but the fungus kills even these shoots after a few years.

If the day comes when there are no more shoots from old stumps, then this tree will be extinct. Nothing we can do will bring it back again.

You will be glad to know that now there are rules that must be followed when plants are imported in an effort to prevent such an accident from happening again.

National Parks Preserve Forests

Whenever we visit a national park, we can see all the plants that live there, if we look long and hard enough. To see all the animals, we have to look very long and very hard—*and* be lucky.

Most animals are likely to run, fly, crawl, or slither away at the first sign of humans. It isn't easy to see what animals are living in a forest, but it's fun to try.

The best way is to sit down, make yourself comfortable, and wait. Squirrels may be the first to appear, scolding you from the safety of a branch high in a tree. Birds may fly close to you, curious about this new visitor on the forest floor. If you are very lucky, a bigger animal may pass by—maybe a raccoon, or even a deer.

ANIMAL TRACKER

American elk were once common throughout much of the United States and Canada. Today they are found only in mountainous parts of the western U.S. and Canada.

American elk are also called "wapiti," a Shawnee Indian name that means "white rump."

These elk are the second-largest type of deer in North America—only the moose is larger. They stand more than five feet tall at the shoulder.

If you were to sit in Olympic National Park, which protects a rain forest in the Pacific Northwest, you might see a herd of Roosevelt elk—and that would really be worth the wait. These magnificent elk became very scarce at the beginning of this century. But now Roosevelt elk are protected from hunters, and their herds are increasing.

Setting aside land for a national park means giving protection to every plant and animal that lives there, allowing them to grow and reproduce. Because all the living things in a forest depend on each other in some way, destroying any part of a forest may harm other parts.

With this in mind, the National Park Service, a bureau of the United States government, prohibits hunting animals, cutting trees, or diverting water from 50 protected natural areas—nearly 46 million acres of nature's most spectacular beauty.

A Tree that Nearly Vanished

In the year 1765 two famous American plant explorers, John Bartram and his son, William, visited the southeastern United States to collect new and interesting plants. In a forest along the banks of the Altamaha River in Georgia they saw an especially beautiful small tree.

This tree has pure white flowers with bright yellow centers. These flowers can be three and a half inches across, and they have a wonderful fragrance. They start to bloom in the summertime, and continue flowering right into the fall. In autumn the leaves of the tree turn a beautiful shade of red.

On this expedition the Bartrams did not see the flowers in bloom, but about a dozen years later William returned and saw the tree covered with white blossoms.

He realized that this tree would be a grand addition to any garden, and brought young plants and seeds back to his own gardens on the banks of a river near Philadelphia. There this new tree grew just as well as it had in its home in Georgia.

This tree had to be given a name. It was named after a famous American, Benjamin Franklin, and after the river near where it was found. Its scientific name is *Franklinia altamaha,* but most people just call it Franklinia.

John Bartram

William Bartram

The plants were seen in the wild for the last time in 1803. Afterward, people searched long and hard, but all the trees were gone, and no one knows why.

All the Franklinia plants now alive are descendants of plants collected in the 1700s. If the Bartrams had not planted Franklinia in their gardens, it would be extinct today. Because these plant explorers collected it, you and I are now able to enjoy its beauty in public gardens. It's even possible to buy Franklinia plants from plant nurseries to grow in your own garden.

Franklinia flowers

The Air Our Forests Breathe

Germany's Black Forest is a land of enchantment. For hundreds of years, people have enjoyed hiking on its timbered hills, skiing on its snowy slopes, and admiring its plants and animals. But in recent years, people have become aware that this enchanted forest is not as healthy as it once was.

The exact reasons for this decline in the health of the Black Forest, and of many others like it in Europe and North America, are not clear. Many natural problems can affect forest trees. Insects and disease, drought and harsh winters, all can injure and even kill trees.

But now there is a new problem—acid rain.

Acid rain is a man-made pollution. It's caused by certain chemicals, mostly from coal-burning power plants and car exhausts, which get into the moisture of the air. These chemicals can make rain and fog acid. In fact, some acid fog is just about as acid as lemon juice!

Acid rain can injure tree leaves and needles when it touches them, and it can change the chemistry of the soil where the trees grow.

Scientists in Europe and North America are studying acid rain. They want to find out just how serious the problem is, but it takes a long time to do careful research.

It's important to find out so that we can make sensible decisions about the best ways to protect our forests.

Acid rain

Acid rain may limit a plant's ability to grow. It can kill tender shoots, and a weakened tree is less able to resist disease and insect attack.

rain cloud containing harmful oxides

to leaves

to soil, lakes, rivers, and ground water

Sulfur and nitrogen oxides released by factories, automobile exhaust, and power stations mix with water in the air to form tiny drops of acid.

Acid rain can release toxic metals such as lead into the soil.

Caretakers for the Earth

We know a lot about the plants and animals that live in tropical rain forests. But there's even more that we *don't* know.

For every plant, animal, or insect of a tropical rain forest that we do know about, there are at least six that we don't.

If the rain forests were to be destroyed, all these unknown forms of life would be destroyed. And the forests *are* being destroyed.

We can't tell exactly how rapidly the forests are being lost, but one estimate is that one or two square miles of forest out of every hundred is cut down every year! In some parts of the world the rate is much, much higher.

BEAK BOX

Toucans have very large beaks. These birds use their beaks to eat berries, fruit, insects, and even small animals. The upper part of the beak is saw-toothed. A toucan holds its food in one foot, and minces it with its beak.

Toucans can be found in forests from southern Mexico through Central America, as well as in northern and eastern parts of South America.

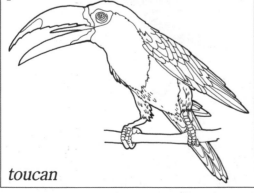

toucan

Rain forests are being cleared for farms, homes, timber, pasture land—for all sorts of human needs. Human needs must be met, but the cost of meeting them by destroying rain forests is unbearably high.

Many people are thinking very hard about this problem, and some solutions are beginning to be understood.

More and more people *want* to save the rain forests. These people feel that humans are caretakers for the earth. They hope that their children's children will share their world with the same plants and animals pictured in this book.

Don't you hope that a coloring book 200 years from now could still show a toucan and a sleepy sloth?

We All Need Forests

Are forests important to you?

You might not be ready to answer that question now, because you've never given it any thought. Think about this:

The paper you're coloring on came from a tree. Think of all the paper you use in a single day—writing paper, magazines, books, paper napkins, cereal boxes, your family's morning newspaper—and imagine how different life would be without these products. Each one was probably made from a tree in a conifer forest of North America.

We rely on hundreds of products that we harvest from trees. Some we use as is, such as fruits and nuts and firewood. Other forest products, such as timber for furniture and building materials, are cut, planed, and sanded into useful shapes.

Many more forest products are made by processing wood chips and sawdust with various chemicals. Paper results from such a process, and so do some plastics, medicines, synthetic fabrics, paints, and soaps.

Now think about this:

When you inhale, your lungs take oxygen from the air. When you exhale, your lungs put carbon dioxide into the air. Plants do the opposite, taking in carbon dioxide and putting out oxygen. We couldn't live without oxygen, and that oxygen comes almost entirely from plants! The forests of the world provide a great deal of the oxygen we breathe.

Some people think that what we need most of all from forests is the variety of plants and animals they support. This diversity helps to keep the whole world healthy.

A lot of people think we need forests most of all because they are so beautiful.

What do you think?

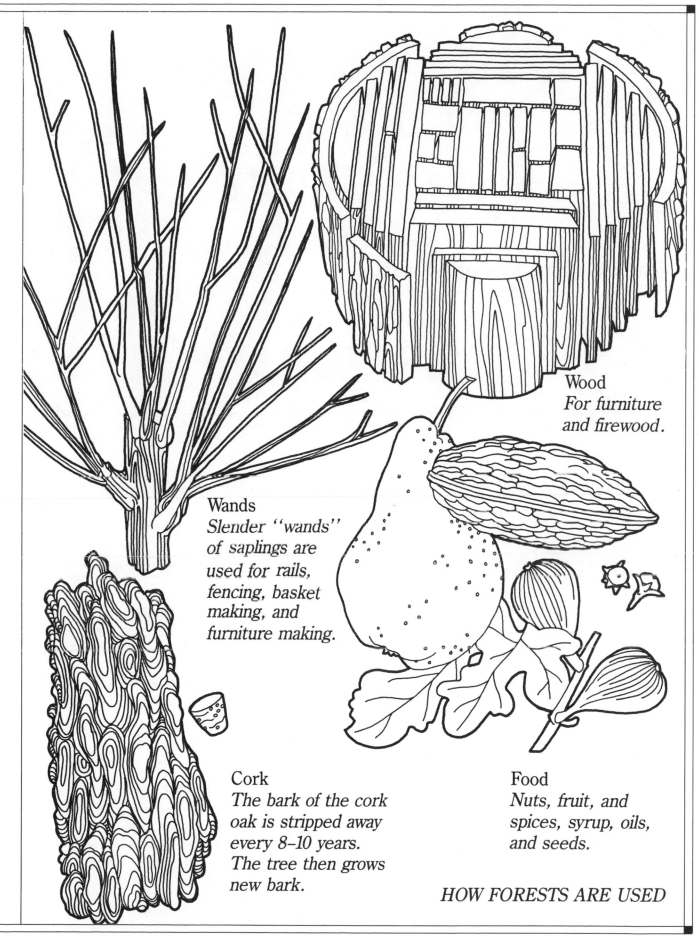

Wood
For furniture
and firewood.

Wands
*Slender "wands"
of saplings are
used for rails,
fencing, basket
making, and
furniture making.*

Cork
*The bark of the cork
oak is stripped away
every 8–10 years.
The tree then grows
new bark.*

Food
*Nuts, fruit, and
spices, syrup, oils,
and seeds.*

HOW FORESTS ARE USED

FOR FURTHER READING

America's Wild Woodlands. W. Howarth. Edited by Donald J. Crump. Washington: National Geographic, 1985. 200 pages. $7.95.
   Covers just about all of our forests.

Familiar Trees of North America: Eastern Region. Audubon Society Pocket Guide. New York: Alfred A. Knopf, 1986. 80 pages.
   Illustrated with photographs of living trees.

A Field Guide to Eastern Forests: North America. Peterson Field Guide Series. John C. Kricher and Gordon Morrison. Boston: Houghton Mifflin, 1988. 512 pages. $22.95 (cloth); $14.95 (paper).
   A book for parents, with lots of good information on forests, including brief descriptions of forest types such as everglades, flood plains, maple, and boreal; ecology; patterns of seasons.

Trees. David Burnie. New York: Alfred A. Knopf, 1988. (One of a series of Eyewitness Books.) 64 pages. $12.95.
   A very nice book, well illustrated with photographs and drawings. Describes the life of a typical tree: growth, leaves, pollination, fruits, pollution, care; includes a few activities.

Trees. Revised edition. A Golden Guide. Herbert S. Zim and Alexander C. Martin. New York: Golden Press, 1987. 160 pages. $3.95.
   A great book to help kids identify trees. Drawings and maps.